the bride of Inglish

the bride of Inglish
Copyright © 1998 Zaffi Gousopoulos
Illustrations © 1998 Ron Edding

Acknowledgments: Several of these poems have seen prior publication in *Contemporary Verse 2, Dandelion, Existere, Ed...Cetera, Rebel Chicks '96*, and the anthology *Making A Difference: Canadian Multicultural Literature* (Oxford University Press), as Ron Edding illustrated postcards (Graphikos Productions), and in the Author's chapbook *The Playing Field* (Insomniac Press). Many of these poems have also been broadcast on CIUT, CHIN, CHSR, CFMT and MuchMusic.

Cover design by Joe Blades based upon b&w illustrations by Ron Edding
Design and in-house editing by Joe Blades
Printed and bound in Canada by Sentinel Printing, Yarmouth NS

No part of this publication may be reproduced, stored in a retrieval system or transmitted, in any form or by any means, without the prior written permission of the publisher or, in the case of photocopying or other reprographic copying, a licence from the Canadian Copyright Licencing Agency (CAN©OPY), 6 Adelaide St East Suite 900, Toronto ON M5C 1H6. Ph (416) 868-1620, 1-800-893-5777.

The Publisher acknowledges support from the Department of Canadian Heritage-Multiculturalism Program for publication of this title, and support from the Canada Council for the Arts-Emerging Publisher program and the New Brunswick Department of Economic Development, Tourism & Culture-Arts Development Branch.

Author photo by Bern Jameson
@ Denise Grant Photography

THE CANADA COUNCIL | LE CONSEIL DES ARTS
FOR THE ARTS | DU CANADA
SINCE 1957 | DEPUIS 1957

Canadian Cataloguing in Publication Data
Gousopoulos, Zaffi, 1967-

    The bride of Inglish

    Poems.
    ISBN 0-921411-70-7

I. Title.

PS8563.O8733B7 1988   C811'.54   C98-950185-X
PR9199.3.G6568B7 1988

Broken Jaw Press
MARITIMES ARTS PROJECTS PRODUCTIONS
Box 596 Stn A
Fredericton NB E3B 5A6   ph / fax 506 454-5127
Canada   jblades@nbnet.nb.ca

the bride of Inglish

Zaffi Gousopoulos

Fredericton • Canada

I would like to thank the following people for their inspiration and support: Andreas Andreopoulos, Nik Beat, Joe Blades, Paul Brundtland, Margaret Christakos, Lynn Crosbie, Ron Edding, Mary Elizabeth Grace, Lisa Jarls, Clifton Joseph, Noah Leznoff, Mike O'Connor, Juan Opitz, K.G. Sambrano, David Sereda, Shafiq, Ann Shin, Rosemary Sullivan and George Tsiosioulas. Very Special Thanks to Elvira.

The Author acknowledges support from the Multiculturalism Program of the Department of Canadian Heritage, and the Ontario Arts Council's Writers' Reserve.

To order the companion CD, *The Queen of Canada*, or to inquire about workshops and booking performances, please write to:
>*Mousiké Productions*
>Box 41092 Bathurst St PO
>Toronto ON M6B 4J6
>Canada

This book is dedicated to Goose and my father

"Mother," he said, "why grudge our loyal bard the right to entertain us as the spirit moves him? Surely it is not the poets that are responsible for what happens, but Zeus himself ... You must be brave and nerve yourself to listen ... So go to your quarters now and attend to your own work, the loom and the spindle ..."
— Homer
translated by E.V. Rieu

I tell you, they have been generous with me, the violet-weaving Muses
— Sappho
translated by Paul Roche

the bride of Inglish

one of us
the basement	13
the Florida children	14
your best friendKristan	16
the Navy Blue Snowsuit	18
the empty bag of Cheesies	19
the taste of chocolate	20
gentlemen prefer blank cheques	22
the bloody white uniform	24
homeland	26
this old man	28
My name is Eleni	31

poetic licence by proxy
the wrath of Grandma Goose	37
Lola	39
the wooden cross	41
the local taverna	42
postcards	43

bare feet
canoe	53
the princess of Malibu mountain	54
beach	56
Monterey	57
the plastic Coke cup	58
the Green Tortoise	59
Mt. St. Helens	61
sleepy in Seattle	63
Bodega Bay	65
the Avenue of the Giants	66
speaking Boontling	

mended with hockey tape
the heartland	73
July 1st	74
Foreign Places	75

The Queen of Canada	77
a perfect match	78
what the cat caught got called good luck	80
the singer	81
the bride of Inglish	82
homefree	84
songbirds	86

one of us

Hue see the stupit Canadian people?
 — my mother, watching *Oprah*

the basement

armoured in black boots
and a thick plaid shirt,
you sneak downstairs
at 6 A.M.
with your secret plan
and BANG! BANG! BANG!

the nuclear family
well-known for blowing up a storm
now and then,
understands your serious passion.
with pro tools and hammers, scientific acumen,
install that pacifying pink insulation

the Greek father building the ideal Canadian basement.

just in case some wicked storyteller
whips our house up over the rainbow,
into the plot of an alien landscape.

y'know, I'll be the one lost from home,
stuck in my pink room
with my poems poems poems;
until I wake up in some strange New World
bust open that door
saying *gosh*,
I don't think I'm in Willowdale
anymore.

the Florida children

three kids in Clearwater Beach
dressed up in their new tanned skin,
all under the aegis of magic sea shells
and the age of 16,
walk the plank boardwalk
muzzled by shiny sports cars,
a band of palm trees shaking their floppy wigs.
lips smack on their knotted wrists,
sucking up runaway drops
of soft-serve vanilla ice cream,
crowned with thin toques of chocolate.

down to The Holiday Inn
where local teenagers volleyball on the beach
in white swim shorts and neon bikinis,
stars stuck on their taut tawny skin,
blonde hair a flutter of wings.
some guy with a red pin-striped box of fries
demands *Who Shot JR?*
in plain black courier type
from the cue card of his yellow T-shirt.
trapped in a conspiracy of Hawaiian shorts
and the cult of sea shell jewelry,
tourists sip cocktails on the paved patio
while Kajagoogoo admits *Too Shy*
from the giant speaker,
perched in a palm between three arthritic fingers.

breathing in the breeze as soft and sweet as vanilla,
the three kids finger their lucky sea shells
sunk in the white ear lobes of Adidas.
snow sand cools their feet, gobbled in
to squat like little Buddhas;
the Gulf unrolls licorice
to the lip of the beach,
unseen beneath a blackboard sky
until the swoosh of wet chalk,

dark heads shrink into dark eyes,
clots of dead blood.
blinking back up at that neon green sign:
The Holiday Inn naming itself
with impeccable hindsight
on its blank-faced facade.

and the three Florida children
drugged by the heat of a summer night,
sink beneath their skin, eyes aimed inward:
searchlights burn into old black & white pictures
creased and smudged with fingerprints.
the eyes of their dead people
kick back furious,
shrivelled up, sizzling.

your best friend Kristan

"Suppose you go home now," said Pippy, "so that you can come back tomorrow. Because if you don't go home you can't come back, and that would be a shame."
— Astrid Lindgren

the sun a gold watch
hung from the blue belly of our common god.
telling me it's time to skip rhyming
the sidewalk down to your house
with rubber-band jumpsies and a box of paper dolls.
spend two hours in your backyard
making whirlpools in the 4-foot tub,
run shrieking through the sprinkler on the front lawn,
delirious with tears of cold water.
squat on your porch sucking popcycles
while chewing pink-flavoured gum,
watch the boys play street hockey with dirty tennis balls
bouncing into parked cars,
heat up a can of Alphaghetties for lunch
in your mother's yellow kitchen.

slumber parties in your basement with the weekend rituals:
try on the latest lingerie and wedding rings
from the annual gloss catalogues of
Simpsons and Consumers Distributing;
practice our future kisses on the covers of *Teen Beat Magazine*,
prod into the dark forests of Nancy Drew Mysteries.
then cruise with the stars
on *The Love Boat* and *Fantasy Island*,
hands dunked into a barrel of buttered popcorn;
our young maiden smiles
hid behind Maple Leaf hot dogs.
two giggle-girls between blankets & pillows
wondering what it's like to be a woman.

remember we were the local superheroes.
you Boy Wonder in a light blue T-shirt
and brown corduroy knickers
poised beneath the crab apple tree
pondering the inexplicable,
while I spun on my heels into Wonder Woman.
every summer I lose you for 3 weeks
to the holiday of Myrtle Beach,
the beige trailer we'd camp in parked on the driveway,
gave room to your brother's new blue Gremlin.

at 14 we sneak downtown
to the dangerous streets of Dundas & Yonge,
the forbidden ground
where all the bad people are,
that's what my mother said, and you
believed her.

O Kristan I have to admit it:
I never forgave your cousin for crying like a moron
at the Rick Springfield concert,
even though she warned us two weeks in advance
when we bought the tickets.
she never returned my books by Erma Bombeck
and Judy Blume,
or my paperback bible of *Pippy Longstocking*
and her parables of unspeakable truths.
she never understood
what your best friend knew:
you said you would have no children
when you heard intercourse
kinda hurt,
and childbirth no catalogue picture.

I gave you a black purse for your 16th birthday:
long spaghetti straps hung straight
like swing set chains;
a second heart stuffed with Kleenex,
cherry lip gloss and blue eye shadow —
the first symptoms of serious femininity.

The Navy Blue Snowsuit

the swish swish of nylon snowsuits
smear the empty pages of suburban streets.
mittens stuck in the wee slots
of plastic blue Magic Carpets,
riding the snow behind them

to the local park.
where they zoom down the hill
waving scarves and single arms;
a symphony of shrieks and giggles,
joy bleeding from their eyes.

one day the Navy Blue Snowsuit
shows up with the real toboggan.

with obscene classroom silence
they beam at their crappy Magic Carpets

does the fat-ass Navy Blue Snowsuit
believe in *sharezies*?

when he zooms down the hill for the umpteenth time
past the slack refereeing pine trees,
into the tangled, tragic arms
of a weeping willow
and busts his brand new pine wood toboggan ...

boys and girls,
who liked this story?
raise your hands.
good!
now, when you go back to your seat,
I want you to draw a nice picture.
don't forget to write your name.

the empty bag of Cheesies

you on the small screen
in blue jean bell bottoms and purple scarves
cracking some hilarious joke
about your fat thighs
while Brenda cracks open a Twinkie box.

me on the velvet couch
spitting Cheesies from my orange mouth
while the bag spills its sorry life
on the moss green carpet
and mamá sings opera.

y'know one day I'll grow up
and leave my parents' home.
move to a good job in New Jersey
then ditz 'em,
get my own t.v. show!

come back running through the subways of T.O.
in my black beret and winter coat,
catch the last train north, get home
just in time to marry some nice Greek boy.
from a good family of course.

god forbid they end up a scuffed photograph
in the kitchen drawer.

but Rhoda never gives up hope,
you go on trading anecdotes
with Carlton buzzing ya
from the front door.

and me
the Greek girl
with the empty bag of Cheesies,
spilling her orange voice.

the taste of chocolate

one Easter
mother wouldn't let me
take Holy Communion,
my sad condition
as a bleeding female
lamented over Turkish coffee
with her bitter girlfriends

she said
you're still fasting,
but minus the Lord's blessing
I was screwed for the fiscal year:
so ham & cheese omelettes
and lots of dark chocolate.
my brothers with bread
and strawberry jam
up to their blinky eyeballs,
they threw like ping pongs
when I walked into the room

Good Friday
I stood alone on the sideline
while everyone ducked the epitáphio,
walking by me
chewing chunks of God

that holy night I sat in the aisle
studying my Calorie Counter,
a tiny book bought
for 99¢ at Miracle Mart.
pass the old wicker basket of bucks
then rise to sing Kyrie Eleison,
wiping the good book on my brow

the next morning I watched them
gulp baby spoons of blood;
kiss the Priest's hand
then take a walk
down plush red carpet

standing there the whole time
beneath a fresco of Jesus Christ,
with the taste of chocolate bunnies
dripping
from my mouth

epitáphio: a table decorated with red and white carnations, symbolizing the tomb of Jesus.

gentlemen prefer blank cheques

unbuckle the summer sky,
belly bulge
a light blue T-shirt.

sucking on Maple Leaf jumbo wieners,
the boys back from Troy
anchored around the gas barbeque
by white sock and sneaker.

the women sealed in the kitchen
cutting up cherry cheesecake,
smile through the glass doors
at our beloved heroes
now debating in professional English
the comparative profiles
of sprinkler systems.

a few yards away
on the immaculate green grass,
propped up for the full frontal panoramic mega 3-D special effect:
the artsy-fartsy
unmarried and loveless
in spite of her little black dress,
smoking it up in the arms
of a plastic white lawn chair
from Canadian Tire's spring/summer catalogue.

deal made
she draws a blank face
beneath a veil of black hair
stares at that crooked fence;
cranks off her neck and opens her head
nodding in complete agreement with the FM radio.

the artsy-fartsy wrapped in the ribbon of her dumb hair,
passports to the back seat of a Buick Skylark
where she learns the unearned salary of her self.
up to her nose in who knows what's best
and down to her last 2¢,
says
she in fact prefers gentlemen
who can take the check

point-blank

the bloody white uniform

in your white uniform
smeared with the blood of chickens,
you barge in babbling of
fungi and micro-organisms
such as yeast & bacteria

between your enthusiasm
and my bilingual *Oxford Dictionary*,
we coax the scientific names
into your spiral-bound notebook,
á là phonetic Greek

sprawled on my white rug
you imitate the snot-nosed federal officer
who barged into class
and stared down the kitchen staff
from the podium of his posture

then you got up and told him off
in the official tongue,
your homemade dialect;
those poor foreigners blinking beside you
and none-the-wiser

you giddy school girl
you're gonna show them all
you ain't no *dum dum*

how many times in my mouthy lifetime
you vetoed this foreign tongue.
now on the verge of 60
you sit at the kitchen altar
in your bloody white uniform,
romancing federal policies

your beloved hubby
giggling at Pepe Le Pew,
compared to fungi and micro-organisms
such as yeast & bacteria

you giddy school girl
decked out in your bloody white uniform

for the love of English

homeland

Friday nights throughout the stealthy winter months
they come to the bouzoukia
for the tastes and sounds of their lost homeland

and curse in their mother tongue
Canadians and their coloured money
and their lousy English songs

they curse those that comes to this country
with funny customs and demonic gods,
who ruin the schools the suburbs
the economy

those *mawvre* they come here for money,
but the 4 Greek men
came for nothing.

another round of Metaxas
they hit the dance floor,
doing the zembekiko to a modern song.
laughing at their own banter of cunning metaphors
they order out loud:
20 plates and a marinated octopus,
their black eyes flying into my mouth

a hundred dollars
smashed at the crazy mathematics of rubber feet,
you poor Greeks
with fists full of twenties,
haggled for 2-dollar bills to throw at each other dancing,
arms spread like tipsy branches

all that god awful coloured money falling around you
all that cursed Canadian money
falling to the floor,
covered by broken plates and shoe prints
and the residue of Rothmans tobacco.

all that for the musicians
who sweep the dance floor
then squat like youthful pigeons;
when the 4 Greek men
have finally gone home.

bouzoukia: Greek nightclub with live music
mawvre: derogatory word for people of colour
zembekiko: a traditional solo dance based on improv

this old man

my father's shoes
tumbling in that battered suitcase
knock knock with somersaults.
how many times has he told this story
so I could tell it even better now,
make those heels knock knock so loud
like the knuckled fists of his foreign tongue.
and sing that song he sang by heart
when he crossed that water
the man so proud.
that day he left his native land
to come to this one
so cold and young,
with his head full of thick black hair
and his dream of a million bucks.

why is his story not good enough?
same old stereotype you've heard before.
when I can tell it so much better now
than the one with knack in this old dumb show.
who went to the very first door he saw
and started to knock on wood knock knock.
I can still hear him in spite of the time
lost with 30 years that walked him by.
he said *my Got — I'm gonna be sambody*,
but nobody heard him or blinked an eye.
and he swore back then as he swears so now
he'll never go back to that land
where he dreamed so much.
here was his chance for a better life,
in this country he called O Canadás.

who is this man who weeps
with his head held down
on that old torn couch.
who is this man who limps around
and clanks his shoes at the crack of dawn;
who seeks revenge against the evil god
the ghost of Hamlet with his knock knock.
like the foolish king who lost his crown,
he tells the truth when he lies too much.

this man who talks of love
but moves his lips to a different song.
this man with his brutal eyes
that leer and sneer and knock me out.
this man who wouldn't give me a buck
who'd rather see me starve
and like him suffer and toughen up.
this man who had me somersault
when I heard his key in the broken lock.
this old man who played knick knack
his fist in my heart,
this man whom I say that I cannot love.

that man who'd pepper my tongue
now makes me taste the pain of his salt.
and the bars of soap he tried to plunge
in my dirty mouth,
I now use to wash these memories off.

what is this man but a little soft
with all the years that wore him down.
what is this man since the day he woke up
and he couldn't speak his English tongue.
who tells the story with a broken one
the very first day the doctor sat down
and told him dear Théo, you can't go back now.
I'm sorry my friend, you've lost your luck.

and the sound of his shoes
knock knock in this house,
the shoes that he wears to spite us all.
and the noise he makes
to fix that lock,
or build whatever broke in his heart.

what is this man but a broken clock
that ticks away and talks talks talks.
what is this man when his kids grow up
and leave him lonely on that old stone couch.
what is this man who can't use the tongue
he taught himself and treasured so much.
what is this man but a symbol of us
who can't tell the time when we've had enough.

and what is he when he goes back now
to his native land that shooed him off,
but a small hurt child to his mother's arms.
and they spit their spiteful eyes:
you're not one of us.
you're an *American* you have a better life.
you're an *American* and you have it all.

who is this man who curses his life
says *Got! you goddamn Got!*
I wando die
I wando die

and what is he now
but the truth of a liar,
who once had a dream —
and woke up without it.

My name is Eleni

Allo, my name is Eleni hue-know, lie dat woman in dat krazy story with Paris and Meleneus. She do very bat thing lie, make fighting do her husbant but — she wuz so beautiful.

I don look too goot today, I need to cutting my hair is so terrible. I juz making baby thaz hwhy I so fatso I eating too much ice cream hue-know: Hagen Daz I buy for me from Luflaws, I luf dat store is so nice. Hue-know, do my village? Hwe don half supermarket. An hwe don half too much money.

My husbant Nikos, he come do my country, he toll my fadher he luf me. Come do Kanada he say he wando marrying me but — I so young an, I don wando leaf my family but — dey say *Eleni*: don be stupit. Hyourl life — so goot — to Kanada.

Hue-know, is no eazy do come do dis country, everything so diffrent an too many people no speak Inglish. But I go do school, an I make frient do the other immigrant from China an India an Africa, an all dis country I — I don knowing but, dey taking picture an dey showing do me. An der country look so beautiful.

Ah school, I meeting dis woman Annie she from Polish. Hwe go do coffee an hwe make tolking, an she toll me she lespian ... I laughing becose — do my country? Hwe don half lespian. Greeks? Dey say is — no right.

But deese woman, she wuz so nice, an very zmart, an she take me do a bar an hwe dancing all night .. an ... she try to kiss me ... an I lie ker very much but — my husbant Nikos? He don lie kit. He taking a letter she write me an — he gut so mat, an he do very bad thing to me, so terrible an ... he don let me go do school no more an ... I wash movie an I tolk lie kan actress! no lie Kirene Pappas I hate her she so stupit but ... my husbant Nikos? He say I so kooko but, I juz try to learn Inglish an the t.v. help me.

I make colling to my frient an she say Eleni: hue go do social service. Hue go do woman shelter. Hue go do krisis center an, dey will help hue but ... I candoo dis, dis is terrible. Hue cando dis do my country hue, hue stupit

Kanadian. Hue don know Greek people. An hue don help me. Hue don help me.

I make colling to my odher frient, an she say Eleni: hue a whoite woman; hyourl life — is so eazy. An dis is so stupit becose I no different. I come to dis country an I don speak Inglish, but I go do school an I make typing so goot, an I try do take chub but dey don wanting me. Dey toll me I half no sperience, but dey taking dis woman I know she don know how do typing. But she wuz a "visible minority" an — daz hwhy. An hue Kanadian half hyourl policy. An dis is no right. Dis is no right.

I wando go back to Greece, I wando see my family, I missing dem too much but ... my husbant Nikos? He don lie kit. He toll me Kanada is my country now an ... hwe don half too much money ... I don know hwhat do doing. I make colling do my fadher an I toll him: Nikos is nut a goot husbant do me. An he gut so mat. An he say very bat thing do me. An he colling me poutána, he toll me come do Kanada. He toll me my life — so goot — do Kanada.

An hue say Eleni: hue lie Kreek foot? Hue lie Kreek music? An dancing an hwe Greeks so happy people, an hwe speak Greek so beautiful but ... my son Yanni, he 7, grey 3 now. He toll me his frients make laughing I speak a funny Inglish, an he don wando learn my langwich. I speak Greek do him, an he speak Inglish. An my husbant Nikos? He don speak Greek do me. He speak Inglish. An I no undrastraning him. An he laughing he say Eleni: hue so stupit. But I no stupit. I no stupit.

An I go do immigration. An dey say Eleni: hwe goddo chain jour name to Hell-en. An hwe gonna make hue — Kanadian citizen.

Hwell my name is Eleni:
I no gonna chain-git to Helen

MY NAME IS ELENI ...

poetic licence by proxy

*I said I'm going to leave. Now. With whatever: my travel sack
on my shoulder, a guidebook in my pocket,
my camera in hand. Deep into the soil
and deep into my body I will go to find out who I am.*
    — Odysseas Elytis
    translated by Zaffi Gousopoulos

the wrath of Grandma Goose

On the blue-rimmed balcony, sipping coffee with the afternoon silence; everyone else dozing off in shaded bedrooms.

Below on the patio, hidden by a canopy of grape leaves: a chorus of Greek women; led by Grandma with astonishing seriousness, discussing the size of my pitiful breasts.

Listen to them sing that clever Greek rhetoric that made our ancestors *so* famous: this is what they must have sounded like, the wise ones in the markets of Athens, bantering about the day's pressing issues. Just about to get up when the ladies reach a verdict. They conclude that my breasts are nothing but the foreign-born descendants of my great grandmother Dthéspina — the one Grandma Goose wanted me named after. My whole life leading up to this moment, suddenly it all made sense: cursed by granny for my mother's transgression — my breasts shrunk to a mere handful — symbols of an old grudge I've paid too dearly for.

Back home: *I COULD HAVE BEEN A KNOCK-OUT IF YOU HADN'T INSPIRED THE WRATH OF GRANDMA GOOSE.* My mother protests but I wave her silent. Remind her what she used to tell me: the old woman bent over my sleeping body, spitting and cursing. I tell her how granny would gaze at my limp nightgown; rip open her black dress, boasting how beautiful they were — once upon a time. Running after me, begging to kiss my breasts. To possess them, as she once possessed her mother's — I guess. Or was it her guilty conscience? Loving the ruins of the birthright she deprived me of. Everyone staring at me, titillated with sadness.

In the privacy of the guest bedroom, I would transform into the many-breasted statue of Artemis: suckling my entire female clan, simultaneously...

They pity me, the women in my family: womanhood made to measure, I so obviously lacking. How strange I must have looked getting off the plane, pulling my bulging suitcase, completely breastless. It's a wonder they recognized me at all. Ah, my lovely kinfolk. I confess: lots of Americánas sell their tits and make a stinking fortune — how do you think

I paid for this trip, *mmm*? But they just stare and sympathize, y'know how it is.

So relieved when I meet my Athenian cousin. Her boobs, kept to a minimum, by god gave her the power to learn both French and English.

O Christina
your silk shirts
on your skin so loose

how you validate
this minimalist
Greek-speaking moose

theorizing
back in Canada
though a bit obtuse

what your mother must have done
to inspire the wrath
of Grandma
Goose

Lola

early mornings on the shaded patio
after running across the agorá,
I'd sit and breathe in the music of flowers
from our garden beside the neighbour's house;
her sweet voice from the basement window,
behind the laurel's dark ribbed trunk.

a whole month snuck by in my uncle's house
before I met the girl with the morning songs;
but she would never say what she sings about
to the flowers in her cradled arms.
I heard the story from the local women
on the patio over late morning coffee,
their voices shrunk into a shrill hush:

she was a young girl who fell in love
with a brown-eyed boy from another town;
she was another girl who committed the crime —
broke the sacred seal of her father's pride.
when he found out about his daughter's lust
and her dirty unborn child,
he broke a thick branch off the laurel
on her head many many times,
then down she went into the basement
to the rest of her life.

singing from her bedroom window
while her father lurked outside,
behind the white sheets flapping
on the roof of his father's house.
singing from her basement window
while her father with his insect eyes,
watched me staring at the silent flowers,
and bay leaves falling down.

the wooden cross

on the mountain top
a white life-size
wooden cross;
a young guard
in gazebo lookout
with his black rifle

waits for envious rivals
who sneak up
with tortured hearts
to burn the ancient pine
that couch Kavala
in a picturesque shot

white houses
with flat red roof tops
lined along the mountain,
an open matchbox
for the guddy
gods

the local taverna

down at the local taverna
huddled around a wooden table
in our wobbly braided chairs,
we dip fresh bread into feta
melted over sliced tomatoes
with olive oil and sweet black pepper,
in a crinkled tinfoil bed

the 4 dark men at the other table
creaking in their wooden chairs,
pour baby bottles of ouzo into glasses
while stroking a thick mustache;
the smoke of Turkish cigarettes
wreathing in the hot night air

then off the hinges on that wobbly wall
comes down the bouzouki and the baglama,
one stomping shoe on the ground
someone starts wailing
Ahmaaan! Ahmaaan!

improvise the words of an old song
someone wrote before my parents
were young:
a girl who thiefed her lover's heart
like a leather wallet from his white shirt's pouch

right off the cobbled roads
wanders in a large brown mutt,
wagging his shaggy tail
dripping saliva,
licks a piece of meat
in my uncle's outstretched palm

Ahmaaan! Ahmaaan!

Aman!: melismatic vocals were used by singers as they improvised more verses in old rembetika songs, circa 1920s

Postcards

Zoom up and around the mountain, your black motorcycle on the stretch of an ancient Slinky. Pass pilgrims in baseball caps, a couple of punch buggy taxi cabs; le garçon waiting for Godot in the empty restaurant. Armies of Hellenic flags guard the T-shirt stands while sales clerks belt the daily specials, an international medley of price tags, cheap languages.

Park in the shade of a small tree, slide off the seat, my legs a sticky Band-Aid. 3000 drachmas for a glossy ticket stuffed in the pocket of my purple shorts, mumbling *Drink Coca-Cola*. Walk up the hill and across the marble threshold; my big toes peek-a-booing from the harness of black sandals.

Sun spits up on its blue bib, drips all over the Acropolis its monstrous mouthful of light. Warm winds coming at me from all sides, pushing me around, dance steps smeared in amber dust. You telling your teacher's truth about the gods in sprint Hellenicá, I translate backwards through the roots of my English, double-duty paradox. 2000 foreign tongues and a Texan accent, echoing all around us.

Leaning over the stone wall, we scrutinize the Dionysius theatre, like the real face of a famous person after how many pictures? The audience of white stones trapped in their seats for eternity, taper into a giant megaphone for the earth's protocol. Someone streaks across the dancefloor, I swear it's me in drag: arms thrown up, arguing a belated point with Euripides.

Backstage, the sky a blue jay cloth soaking up sun: I'm telling you — the perfect postcard. This bird's-eye view of history breaks the rhythm of my photo album: plastic pages of drunken relatives, upstaged by the glory that *was* Greek food.

In front of the Parthenon: leaning back on thick twine, suspenders looped around bare arms, my hair a ripped black parachute. Caged inside the temple, in lieu of the missing Goddess: the huge crane with its mouth agape, a New Age dinosaur; poetic license by proxy.

3000 drachmas later, we're gazing at Cretan frescoes; peering into showcases of bronze weapons and gold jewelry. Glass cupboards lined up in highschool geometry, clay pots mended with crazy glue. The German tour guide pointing to a slab of brown stone, the Linear B boustrophedon: capitals of proto-Greek doing laps all the way down to the deep end. I suddenly realize we're the only ones speaking Greek, slapping my voice so I can hear you: quizzing me on the phonetic differences between French & Spanish.

Poseidon with a make-believe pike in the stretch of his metric arms, ready to spear a woman's heart. The bull-headed satyr bent over smirking into Aphrodite's navel: her left hand a fig leaf; sandal raised in her right hand ready to smack him. The white statue of Hermes smirking at something way over our heads.

Later, we take a break, sipping sweet frappe in Plaka, crowded out by the bubble-head smoke of our cigarettes. Bent forward, praising the Hellenic Spirit: the rise and fall of your voice a perfect metaphor.

Leaning back, you ask about my homeland: I plunge into a lively narrative punctured by silence and nervous laughter. Then suddenly you speak fluent English . . .

... reinvent the veil of blonde hair draped over a mysterious paperback, right behind me. The dark-eyed Dorians behind you, leering at me the whole time. "American women are stupid," being your last comment.

Panayoti, I was lucky to meet you. Taking me across the city on that summer day: Parliament Buildings, Universities, all the way out to the new Olympic Stadium. Back in the obscene reality of downtown Athens: the Parthenon, escaped from the postcard, restored on its biblical mountain. Right at the end of that spooky street, lined with kiosks and motorcycles.

Now on this suburban road, slowed down by the pull of my blue wool coat, smearing boot prints in dusty snow. Just over the hill, on the other side of the highway, **The Bay** sign blinks in a pool of grey fog, surrounded by empty parking lots. I'm telling you — the perfect postcard.

bare feet

Just remember, we're all in this alone.
　　—Lily Tomlin

canoe

we'll meet again
some day my friend
one sunny afternoon

right out there
on Venice Canal
in a honking huge blow-up
bright lemon canoe

you'll lie down
with a bottle of wine
and dip your big bruised toe,
then one by one
pluck the eyelids off
a tulip beyond its bloom

I'll sit up straight
and stroke stroke away
around your neighbourhood,
then one by one
with my lifesaver on
belt out some country tunes

and who knows who
and who knows what
we'll find that afternoon

we cruise the Venice Canal
into some new point of view

the princess of Malibu mountain

they say she was a nice girl
with a sweet apple smile
and a normal childhood.
grew up on a pig farm in South Dakota
then came out West for a bit of sunshine,
with a suitcase full of nothing
but Woody Guthrie on vinyl,
and a dustmop of wild flowers

they say he was a real charmer
with a big *snawza*
and a passion for lying.
grew up in a foreign country
where the people talk funny,
and never once saw *Star Wars*

they say he found her asleep
on Santa Monica beach
trapped in a black bikini;
wooed her with a homey song
on his trick guitar
then brought her back
to his castle on Malibu mountain,
where he grows wild flowers,
and guards her beastly beauty

O princess I tried to find you.
the road along the mountain
a dragon's tongue
that never reached the top.
I gave up and went back to Starbucks
for another cup of coffee,
where the locals kept on talking
talking
talking ...

some say she loved him ...
some say ...... mmm ...
some say she died giving birth to an ugly monster ...
some say she found her way back home ...

but nobody knows for sure at all,
what ever happened to ...
the princess ... of Malibu mountain

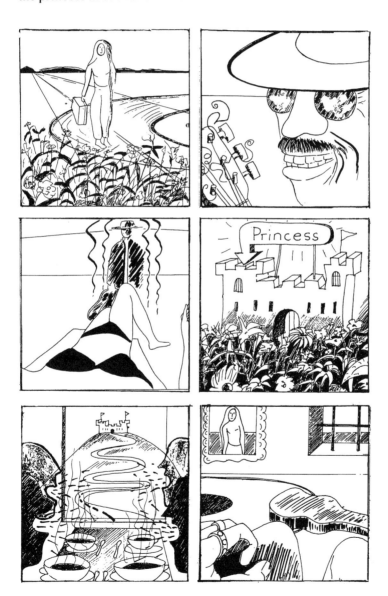

beach

that afternoon at the beach
slapping the sand with our bare feet,
leaps beyond the reach of the yellow Frisbee
taken by the fast-hand breeze.
waves rolling in their wide white lips
to a new age of music,
the moody blues of the old Pacific
licking our ice-creamed skin.
the sky a blue towel
stretched out for miles,
slowly enfolding us in its mother arms.

that afternoon at the beach
smacking off sea kelp stuck to my knee,
hurled into flight on its floppy limbs
and me shrieking some dumb girl on t.v.
you dripping into wet towels
beneath the reign of blue sky
streaked fuzzy by heat waves
of an earthbound sun,
beaming the face of a good god.

that afternoon at the beach
dunking a box of low fat Triscuits
and a bag of burgundy cherries;
life's little stories with songs and poetry.
the joys and pains of real living, the unseen,
flying from our mouths wild swallows
taken by a summer's ease.
the ocean a blue blanket
bundled below our feet,
we reached down pulled up dreaming,
drowned swimming in our nappy sleep.

Monterey
— for Mary Elizabeth Grace

I spent the day in Monterey
where groves of cypress grow,
bend their limbs
to the limber whims
the ways the winds
may blow

I spent the day in Monterey
where cypress make tableaux,
freeze the ways
that show such pains
and time must have
them hold

I spent the day in Monterey
where cypress say they show:
we cannot hide
the truths that lie
inside the shape
of soul

the plastic Coke cup

Time Square
a flock of pigeons
hustle for a bit of bread

some boy stands alone on the corner
a plastic Coke cup
in his hand

shadow of a palm tree
in the store window
behind his small black head

feet still on a red box
doing the robot dance
for a bit of change

I said *hey boy,*
can I take a picture?
you looking better then them billboard ads

and he said
jingle jingle
jingle jingle,
the boy with a plastic hand

The Green Tortoise
— in the memory of Jenn Haberman

I said
one-way ticket to Portland please
pick me up at the Berkeley Marina

if some guy with a speedy smile
bragging bogus luck
tried to talk me out,
I'd say
listen up dude I ain't no fool for a faster route
when the getting's no good.
I'd say
no way going on the Greyhound baby
I wanna feel every thumpy bump;
I wanna go slow on The Green Tortoise man
I wanna ride all night
on the hippie bus

where you can sit at the table with the friendly folk
and trip it way out man crack a few good jokes.
you can play a bit of poker and score a few points
with a bag of pretzels and a bottle of Coke.
you can snuggle up at the back of the bus
high up on a bunk with the guy from New York
and go thumpy bump,
on The Green Tortoise man
on the hippie bus

I said
one-way ticket to Portland please
pick me up at the Berkeley Marina

if some guy with a speedy smile
bragging bogus luck
tries to talk you out,
whadya gonna say?

you say
no way going on the Greyhound baby
I wanna feel every thumpy bump;
I wanna go slow on The Green Tortoise man
I wanna ride all night
on the hippie bus

Mt. St. Helens
— for Katy Morgan

someone stuffed the sky with fluff
from their empty pocket.
we drove our silence through a drizzle of dust
that clanked in the bottom of our eyes.

sucked into the forest's dark mouth,
we cranked the windows up,
radio coughed off.

across the threshold
the shock of sudden light,
thrown into us buckets of cold water.
headless trees scorched black & white,
guard with stubby arm-guns
their 15 years of dead life.
on the other side
two mountains sunk in a muggy sky,
green stubble pimpled with rock.

the mountain abandoned beside you
a giant skull;
I climb up slapping off gravel dust
the texture of whole wheat flour.
ride the rocks down, stumbling,
palms a criss-cross of blood.
no clicky cameras or people talk
as winds wail their three-voiced song;
dusty sandals cracking up gum-ball ground.

snuggle up beside a log burnt birch-white,
its bizarre new body an alien arm.
gaze across the valley at your bruised grey mouth
clouded with misty afterthoughts
of a job well done.
your missing tongue
barfed into in a pool of black blood,
white logs lined up forever drowning.

staring back across the valley
bruised by fists of light,
my eyes fall into the shadows of a rock:
peeking out a red flower
defiant with life,
shaking its one wee arm at you,
fist full up

sleepy in Seattle

nothing but rain these past 4 days

late August
beached on a stranger's bed,
snuggled up in the arms
of a blue duvet

sleepy in Seattle
stares out the window
southwest of the cityscape

prays for a bit of blue
to break through,
bust those bubble clouds
and their royal rain

not even that
most excellent cup
of serious latte
can keep her awake

sleepy turns away
from the wet window,
dreams about another place

where the sun swoops down
with its creamy mouth
in the skin of a summer day

sleepy in Seattle
looks up says

thank god
I'm awake

Bodega Bay
— for Ann Shin

one hour
in Bodega Bay
alone on the dizzy docks,
she swallows the blue warmth of sky & water
as the wind shoves its many arms

one hour
in Bodega Bay
she gropes sky's blue cloth
the seagulls slash up with razor flight
then swoop down for their hungry lunch

one hour
in Bodega Bay
no words to soothe smooth her eyes,
when the winds beat hard
the day falls face down,
and the ocean smacks its mouth

the Avenue of the Giants

shadows creep across the windows,
breathing on your naked arms

the long shot from your Cavalier, looking up:
sun's torn skin
caught in the hair-nets of ancient redwoods,
flickering stars and angel wings.
wrinkled trunks pulled up solid to no visible crotch
lit burgundy brown,
sweet wine seeps through the forest's crunchy carpet

in the Avenue of the Giants
you grow so small,
a black dot in unmapped country,
no name recalled.
hiding your heart in a sweaty palm like stolen gum
your mouth spit out,
teeth glob of sweet gall.
run through their legs laughing you won't get caught,
then catch yourself in the metal of your own trap tongue:

stand beside a tree it would take 6 of you to hug,
head cranked an obscene angle
cuts off your blood,
all thought;
the wisdom of ancient life
falls into your dumb mouth,
explodes swallowed;
a new sun

in the Avenue of the Giants
you spit out your native tongue,
vow to quit cigarettes & writing,
no names to call.
dance to the peaceful poetry of redwood forests
your bare feet soaked burgundy brown

stop
hold out your heart
embarrassed by its stained mouth
melting in the sweat of your palm.
cracks into a faint fluttering
with a gush of blood,
as the redwoods gather a blanket around you,
whispering their new song

speaking Boontling

let's take a trip to Boonville
for a bit of home brew
at the local bar
where the Boonies like to gather
after a long day on the job

we'll sit and listen
like foreign students
and boy we'll learn a lot
cuz the locals they like their homebrew
and *gosh* they love to talk

some strange old local lingo
they play on the English tongue
bamboozle with a bosh of wording
so baffling and confusing,
that buzz of Boontling
makes you wonder who you are,
cuz the locals they got the boon in them
and *gosh* they laugh it up

let's take a trip to Boonville
for a bit of homebrew
and learn to bluff
that same old local lingo
on our foreign English tongue

come home like native Boonies
and boy we'll say a lot
cuz we foreigns we'll have the boon in us
and *gosh* — we gotta talk

Author's note: During the late 19th Century in Boonville (a small town in northern California), a group of children invented a secret version of English. Apparently, this trick evolved into *Boontling*, the local language most often used to beguile outsiders.

mended with hockey tape

I have always been driven by some distant music — a battle hymn, no doubt — for I have been at war from the beginning.
— Bette Davis

the heartland

the stop sign a flag
stabbed in a patch of grass
behind a tree's shadow.

sidewalk cracks
the way veins rip flesh or
wrinkles gouge an old maid's face
when laughing.

the blinky red light of E.T.'s heart
going off on its final countdown
before this genre self-destructs;
squeezing out its bottle mouth:
baby's first good cry.

she turns left,
drives past the pointed arrow
into a no exit,
tires slice through fresh blood

fingers curl
the red legs of a crab on its back;
shakes her up

light blue Chevette
tumbling across a green table

delirious spits of laughter,
thinks he's just won the jackpot.

July 1st

you get a day off
so you stay home curled up
in the safe warmth of pillows and futon,
with your favourite mug full of gourmet coffee

when some fatal bias
has you over-bid by twenty thousand
dollars in the Final Showcase Showdown,
perhaps this is not just another statutory holiday.

trapped in the cheap seats of this foreign country
you have memorized the wrong prices.
I'm afraid you have wasted all your time
and all your money
and all your crappy life

poor thing
alone in the moment
with her measly mug

I swear if I just tried a little harder
I could have won
eh?
y'know,
I could have been

a star

Foreign Places

the old man who thinks we're from the same place
assumes a conversation in his native language
which I regrettably cannot comprehend.
he keeps staring at me nevertheless,
and in between his fits of silence, says
You Jewish? You Italian? You Pakistan?

flings his savage breath in my dear direction
chips the white mask of public space;
then says in perfect CBC anglais,
hey what country you from anyway?

ah, the Trick Question
I failed on the exam;
let's proceed with caution, shall we?

now, we do agree that in this foreign city
everyone is from somewhere else;
we need to know just where that where is at
so we can intellectualize our feelings together
and fight racism,
and get along really well.

well well.

I try to explain to the nice old man I'm quite politely from Willowdale.
north-east of the city proper, I admit it's a mere suburb.
nevertheless a foreign place
to many refugees such as my very self.

the wise old man of course knows better.
with one huff he points his finger up to God:
you better get yourself a good job,
don't marry a mungi-cake they make
bad husbands, and
where are you *really* from?

ah, the Trick Question
trying to fail me once again.

I admit by official standards I am quite a stranger,
somewhat hopelessly ethnic,
a female of exactly Greek descent,
I'm afraid.
nevertheless, I'm going to grow up
and be a Canadian Artist one day,
and man will you regret not having my autograph
cuz I'll be quite famous by then. O Yes.
I'll be so famous I'll look like everyone else.
I'll look like a true Canadian of female descent.
and then how will you ever find me?
and what will you do then? *mm*?

anyway, the old man goes back to his private place
in his country's far-away imagination,
where all the woman look the same
being from the same place
but clearly unCanadian, I'm afraid.
I resume my brilliant absence from being born in this idiot place,
staring out the mythic window
as the streetcar thunders through Queen St. West
towards the dark grey spaceship of winter
entering the foreign city
for a wee visit,
I'm afraid.

The Queen of Canada
— for Mike

when I am The Queen of Canada
I will be the lucky bride,
I'll sit on my throne
reading epic poems
the King's *Bible* by my side

when I am The Queen of Canada
you could be my cutie pie,
run off to war
wherever you go
with me in your loving eyes

when I am The Queen of Canada
we will never have to fight,
with all the gifts
you've given me
I'll have the perfect life:

with my bottle of Coca-Cola
my Charter of Rights
my amulet against the Evil Eye

with my box of figs
my Blue Jay cards
my copy of *Wayne's World*
close to my heart

when I am The Queen of Canada

man will I love my job

a perfect match

her white dress
collapsed into a black lasso
around missing feet.
red roses swelling over three hands, bleeding;
their faces cranked an impossible angle,
the long lines of her see-through veil.

on the flipside of this pack of matches
in the blur of pink italics:
"Joe & Mary"
docked above their June anchor;
spliced a perfect catch.
KEEP AWAY FROM CHILDREN
followed by the French version
picketing the white flap.

flipped up, the maids spring forward
a good Greek chorus,
their mouths scooped out
by song;
white heads burnt black in a poof! of fire.
count the last days until December
from the rulers of your life
as her face melts away into more clichés
and the music ends.
the red bouquet plummets past the bottom line
of her definite dress,
lands across the strip of sulphur,
face full of slash marks.

pick it up when the music starts
the long black lines of my hair go white;
spring forward a garden of roses,
hissing at dirty rocks.

what the cat caught got called good luck

my tongue a pink fish
sliced in half
jerks up to suck its brave last breath
then flops down dead:
hung from my lip
the cat's lucky catch.

what is my tongue
but a brush that pants,
slips up the sleeve of your milky legs
then makes a big splash:
hung from my lip
in the cat's lucky lap.

the singer
— for Kim Doolittle

I tell ya just once
I'll brag to the world
about my mighty vagina
and how it feels so good

I swear it's so true:
this giddy girl
sings her little heart out
like Judy Garland

sweet songs of love
through her mighty lungs
sounds so fucking good man —
and without a mic

the bride of Inglish

"I demand a creature of another sex, but as hideous as myself ... It is true we shall be monsters, cut off from all the world; but on that account we shall be more attached to one another ... Oh! My creator, make me happy ..."
— Mary Shelly

these last days of August
how the sunlight swarms around us,
licks the sweat from our sweetest thoughts

these last few hours of this day's life
suck the old skin off my purple heart,
makes burgundy wine of this bitter blood

these last few words I take into lung
make this poetry my sacred song,
Inglish tongue

candle drips on my sweaty thigh
as I wait
beneath the hot dark mouth of night

for the forbidden fatal kiss of God

It is better to light a candle than to curse the darkness
— Eleanor Roosevelt

homefree

kick up your feet
run run my little friends,
for I am the one
who is IT again.
I promise to close my eyes
and count to 10,
give you a good chance
to run far away.
then ready or not here I come
with my slow shuffle
and stretchy arms.
I'll smile my friends
as I chase you around,
slow down each and every time
so you never get caught.
this game I play
just to see you smile,
hear your laughter
as you go run run,
scrunching gold maple leaves
all around that trunk;
a collage of bright nylons
little hands on bark.
chanting
"trees are homefree!
trees are homefree!"

so kick up your feet
my little friends run run,
for I am the one
who is not so young.
I promise to play
as long as you want,
then end this game ready or not.
so let me see you smile
let me see you smile,
hear your laughter

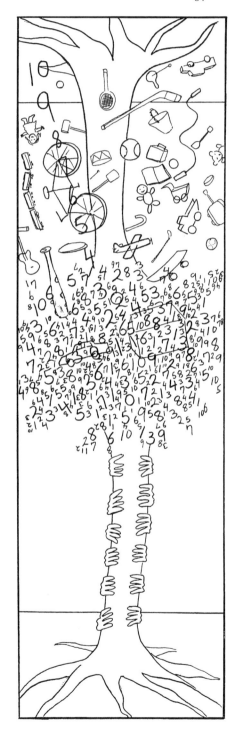

as you go run run,
shrieking at the end of
my long-stretched arms:
trees are homefree,
trees are homefree.

songbirds

some birds just love to dream
spread their given wings
fly far away

some birds just have to leave
brave those mighty winds

and those birds they always say
without any words the ways of their pain

they say one day
what they learn to know,
they wanna go back home
they say, some day.

and this bird? she always said
I'm gonna make my songs
fly me away

I'm gonna leave this place
and never come back
she said, some day.

and this bird she got away
spread her small bruised wings
mended with hockey tape

and crash boom bam
into the empty net,
the knotted web of her lonesome self

and this bird she began to say
without any words the lies of her age

she says one day
what she learns to know,
I wanna go back home ...
I wanna go back home ...
I wanna go back home ...
she said, some day.

and this bird she sings old songs
sets her small bruised wings
and soars with the young

she prays one day
their words will cut

what's bane on the bones

this knot in the heart

A Selection of Our Titles in Print

96 Tears (in my jeans) (Vaughan)	0-921411-65-0	3.95
Best Lack All, The (Schmidt)	0-921411-37-5	12.95
Coils of the Yamuna (Weier)	0-921411-59-6	14.95
Cover Makes a Set (Blades)	0-919957-60-9	8.95
Cranmer (Hawkes)	0-921411-66-9	4.95
Crossroads Cant (Grace, Seabrook, Shafiq, Shin, Blades (ed.))	0-921411-48-0	13.95
Dark Seasons (Trakl; Skelton (trans.))	0-921411-22-7	10.95
for a cappuccino on Bloor (MacLean)	0-921411-74-X	13.95
Gift of Screws (Hannah)	0-921411-56-1	12.95
Heaven of Small Moments (Cooper)	0-921411-79-0	12.95
Herbarium of Souls (Tasić)	0-921411-72-3	14.95
I Hope It Don't Rain Tonight (Igloliorti)	0-921411-57-X	11.95
In the Dark—Poets & Publishing (Blades)	0-921411-62-6	9.95
Invisible Accordion, An (Footman (ed.))	0-921411-38-3	14.95
Like Minds (Friesen)	0-921411-81-2	14.95
Lad from Brantford, A (Richards)	0-921411-25-1	11.95
Longing At Least Is Constant (Payne)	0-921411-68-5	12.95
Notes on drowning (mclennan)	0-921411-75-8	13.95
Open 24 Hours (Burke; Reid; Niskala; Blades, mclennan)	0-921411-64-2	13.95
Poems from the Blue Horizon (mclennan)	0-921411-34-0	3.95
Poems for Little Cataraqui (Folsom)	0-921411-28-6	10.95
Milton Acorn Reading from *More Poems for People.* (Acorn)	0-921411-63-4	9.95
Rant (Fowler-Ferguson)	0-921411-58-8	4.95
Rum River (Fraser)	0-921411-61-8	16.95
Seeing the World with One Eye (Gates)	0-921411-69-3	12.95
Speak! (Larwill; *et al*)	0-921411-45-6	13.95
St Valentine's Day (Footman)	0-921411-45-6	13.95
Strong Winds (Hyland (ed.))	0-921411-60-X	14.95
There are No Limits to How Far the Traveller Can Go (Gates)	0-921411-54-5	4.95
Under the Watchful Eye (Deahl)	0-921411-30-8	11.95
Voir Dire (Flaming)	0-921411-26-X	11.95

Available from **General Distribution Services**, 325 Humber College Blvd, Toronto ON M9W 7C3: Toronto, ph (416) 213-1919, fax (416) 213-1917; Ont/Que 1-800-387-0141; Atlantic/Western Canada 1-800-387-0172; USA 1-800-805-1083. Sales representation by the Literary Press Group of Canada, www.lpg.ca ph 416-483-1321. Direct from the publisher, individual orders must be prepaid. Add $2 shipping for one book ($9.95 and up) and $1 per additional item. Canadian orders must add 7% GST/HST.

MARITIMES ARTS PROJECTS PRODUCTIONS
BOX 506 STN A
FREDERICTON NB E3B 5A6   Ph/fax: 506 454-5127
CANADA   E-mail: jblades@nbnet.nb.ca